Carry it!

Julia Lawson

Photographs by
Peter Millard

Evans Brothers Limited

Look at all this shopping!

I wonder how many bags
we will need to
carry it home!

Have you ever tried carrying peas in a net ...

or milk in a paper bag,

Can YOU make a special bag to carry one of the things in the photographs?
Is your bag strong enough?
Is it big enough?

or eggs in a jar?

When we want to carry things we can use our arms,

our backs,

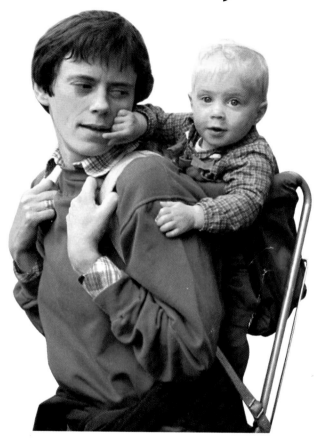

or even our
heads.

Very heavy things need more than one person to carry them.

Gentle snail,
away you go,
I know why you
move so slow;
It must be such
a heavy load,
To carry your
house along
the road.

Light things can also be awkward to carry!

When we have to carry something really big, we need machines to do it for us.

Other things are so small, it is easy to lose them ... even in your pocket!

How many beads can you carry in your hand, in a bag and in a sieve? Try carrying other things too.

How can we carry something

a long, long way?

Pets are very precious, so we have to carry them carefully.

Jump, jump, jump goes the big kangaroo,
I thought there was one, but I see there are two.
The mother takes her young one along in a pouch,
Where it can nap like a child on a couch.

Sometimes we can pack everything into one bag and carry it all together.

"Where shall I put this?"

Notes and suggested activities for parents and teachers

We hope that you have enjoyed sharing this book and have tried out some of the additional ideas found in the activity boxes. Feel free to adapt them as you wish; for example, when you make a bag (pages 6/7), try using different materials, such as paper, card, fabric or a dishcloth. Try making the bag in a range of sizes too.

Storybooks

Listed below are some children's storybooks that relate to the theme of carrying. Have fun!

Handa's Surprise, Eileen Browne, Walker Books
The Lighthouse Keeper's Lunch, Ronda and David Armitage, Andre Deutsch
Carry, Go, Bring, Come Vyanne Samuels, Bodley Head
Mr Gumpy's Outing, John Burningham, Jonathan Cape

Songs

You can sing this to the tune of 'In and Out of the Dusty Bluebells.'

Carry heavy, carry light,
Carry with all your might,
Carry big, carry small,
Carry one and carry all.

Carry fat, carry thin,
Carry all you can fit in,
Carry long, carry tall,
Carry one and carry all.

Choose a range of objects. Pause at the end of each line to allow the children to pick up an item that fits in with the words. Let the children hold up the objects they have chosen as you sing the song again. The children could also pretend to be carrying different objects as you sing the song. Why not let the children make up their own verses too?

Games

Here are some you might like to try.

I Sent a Letter to My Friend
The children should sit in a circle with their eyes closed. They sing:
I sent a letter to my friend and on the way I dropped it.
One of you has picked it up and put it in your pocket.
Is it you? Is it you? It is YOU!

As the children sing, one child walks around the circle and quietly places the letter or parcel behind a child and gently pats him or her on the head. This child then has to get up, pick up the letter and chase the first player around the circle to return the letter.

Mr Wolf's Shopping
One child sits on the floor, eyes closed, surrounded by a range of 'shopping', for example bags or boxes. The other children must creep forward and try to rescue some shopping without alerting 'Mr Wolf'.

If the children find this too easy, try putting some beads inside the boxes or using bags that rustle; the children will have to carry them very carefully to avoid being caught!

Carry It!
This game is great fun and is also very useful in demonstrating social and co-operative skills. Children should work with a partner and carry a variety of objects – balls of different sizes, balloons, boxes etc. – in unusual ways. For example, ask two children to carry a ball between them using:
- their tummies
- without using their hands
- using only their feet
- using one hand.

Video

Channel 4, Stage One: Machines

Index

Photography acknowledgements

page 9: (left) Last Resort Picture Library
        (right) Robert Harding Picture Library
page12: Still Pictures
page14: Still Pictures
page15: Robert Harding Picture Library